It's fun to draw Fairies and Mermaids

Mark Bergin

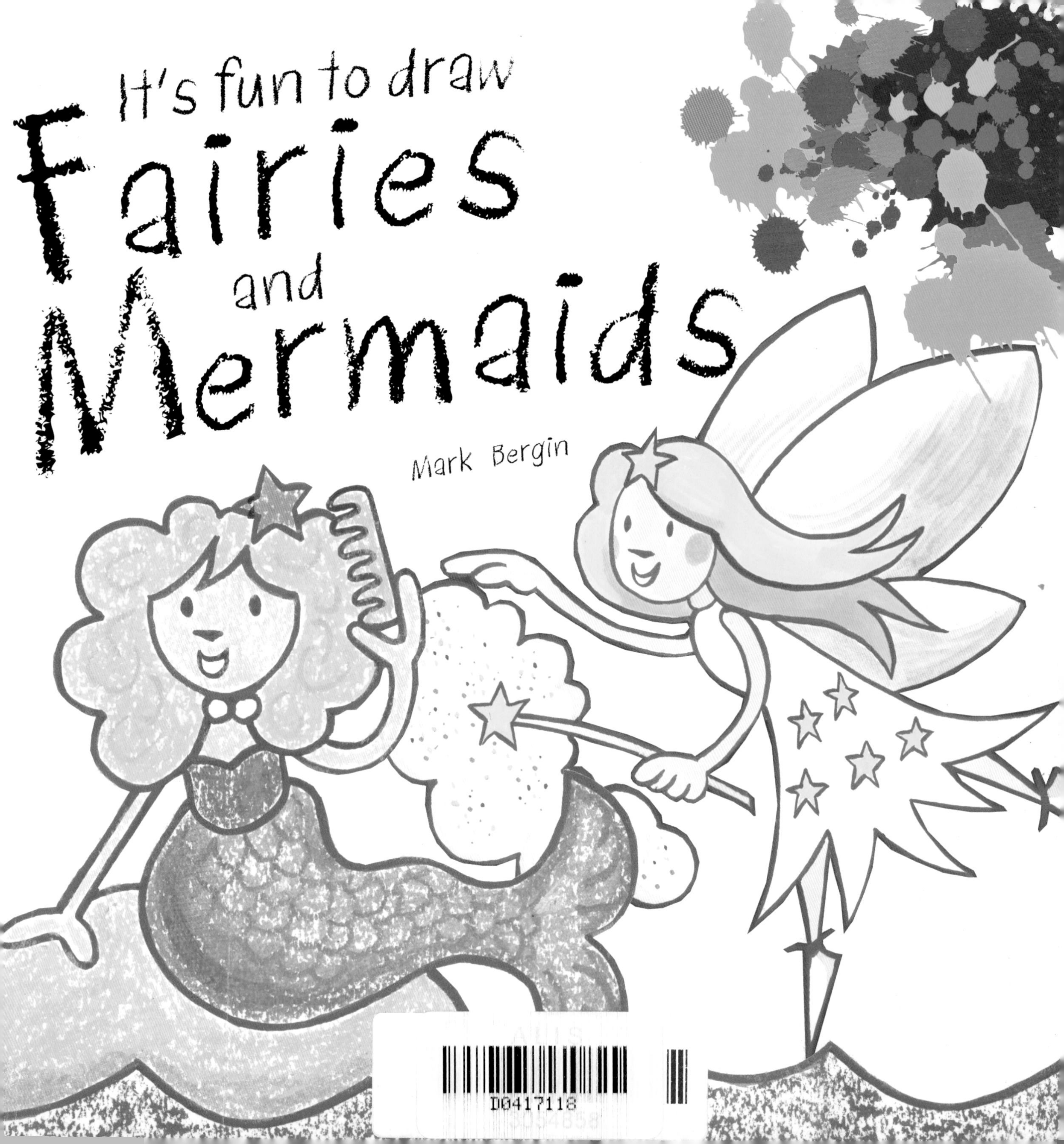

Author:
Mark Bergin was born in Hastings, England. He has illustrated an award winning series and written over twenty books. He has done many book designs, layouts and storyboards in many styles including cartoon for numerous books, posters and adverts. He lives in Bexhill-on-Sea with his wife and three children.

Editorial Assistant:
Rob Walker

HOW TO USE THIS BOOK:
Start by following the numbered splats on the left hand page. These steps will ask you to add some lines to your drawing. The new lines are always drawn in red so you can see how the drawing builds from step to step. Read the 'You can do it!' splats to learn about drawing and colouring techniques you can use.

Published in Great Britain in MMXII by
Book House, an imprint of
The Salariya Book Company Ltd
25 Marlborough Place, Brighton BN1 1UB
www.salariya.com
www.book-house.co.uk

ISBN-13: 978-1-907184-68-0

1 3 5 7 9 8 6 4 2

A CIP catalogue record for this book is available from the British Library.

Printed and bound in China.

Contents

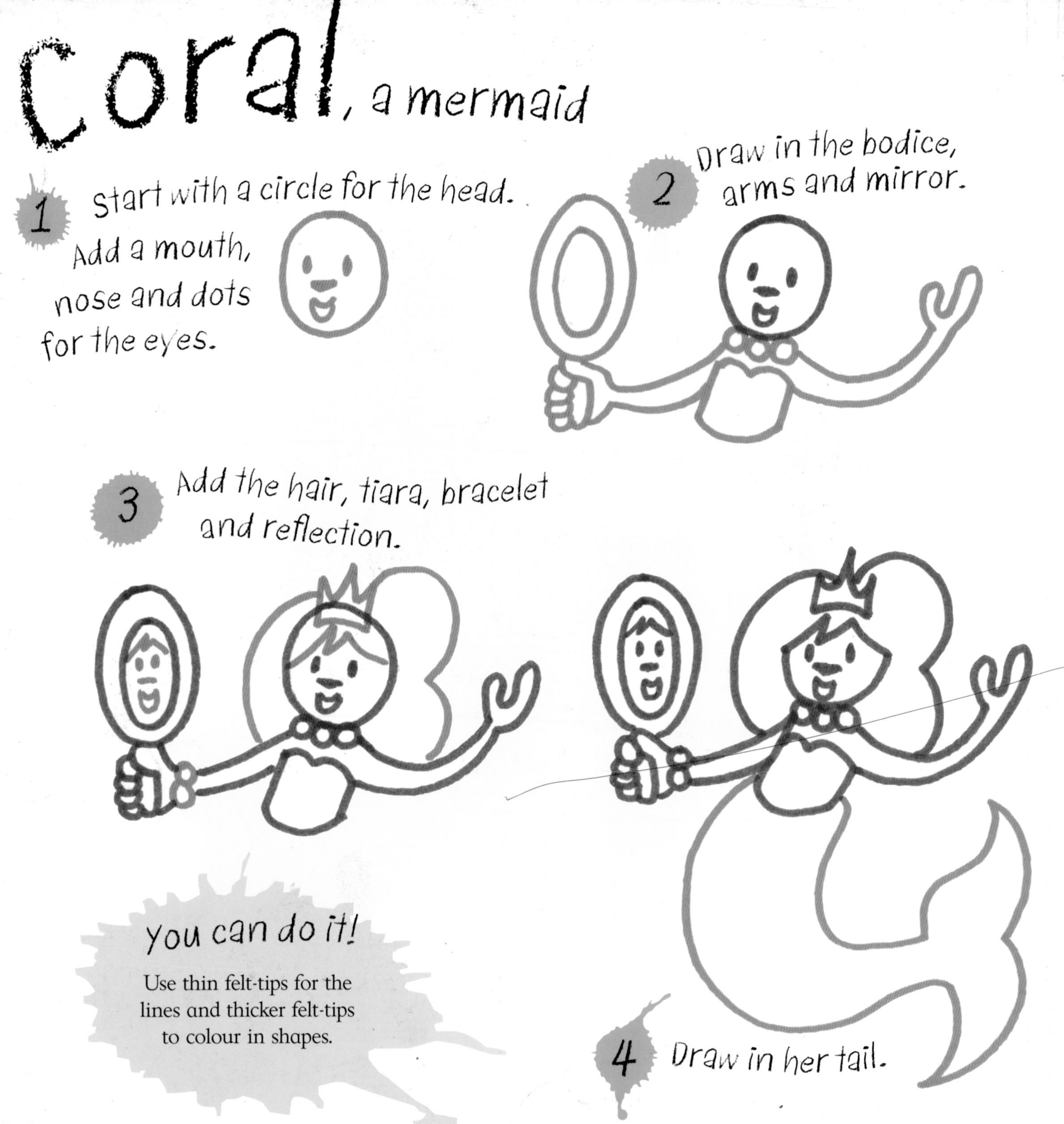
Coral, a mermaid
1 Start with a circle for the head.
Add a mouth, nose and dots for the eyes.
2 Draw in the bodice, arms and mirror.
3 Add the hair, tiara, bracelet and reflection.
you can do it!
Use thin felt-tips for the lines and thicker felt-tips to colour in shapes.
4 Draw in her tail.

Splat-a-fact!

Mermaids are very vain and always carry a mirror and comb.

Buttercup, a fairy

1 Start with the head. Add nose, mouth and dots for eyes.

2 Draw in the dress.

You can do it!

Use a felt-tip for the lines. Add colour with oil pastels. Use your finger to smudge colours.

Splat-a-fact!

Woodland fairies look after the flowers and trees, with the help of the small creatures who live there.

3 Add the arms and legs.

4 Draw in two wings and her hair.

Pearl, a mermaid

1 Start with the head, the mouth and a a dot for the eye.

2 Add the hair and tiara.

You can do it!

Use pencil for the outlines then paint in watercolour. Add coloured inks to the wet paint for texture.

Splat-a-fact!

Mermaids and mermen have lived in the ocean since the beginning of time.

3 Draw in the bodice and arms.

4 Add her tail.

5 Finish the drawing, adding a crab and rock.

Sparkle, the Tooth Fairy
1 Start with the head. Add a mouth, a nose and dots for the eyes.
2 Add the hair.
3 Draw in the dress.
You can do it!
Use felt-tip for the outline. Add colour using wax crayons.
4 Add the arms and legs.
Splat-a-fact!
The tooth fairy collects children's baby teeth and leaves a gift in return.
5 Draw in wings, a wand, and a bow in the hair.

sandy, a mermaid

1 Cut out the head. Add mouth and eye and stick them down.

you can do it!

Cut out the shapes from coloured paper. Stick these on to a sheet of blue paper. Use felt-tip for the lines.

2 Cut out the hair. Stick down.

MAKE SURE YOU GET AN ADULT TO HELP YOU WHEN USING SCISSORS!

3 Cut out the arms and chest. Stick down.

4 Cut out a long green tail, a flower and some beads. Stick down.

Splat-a-fact!

Mermaids often come to the rescue of shipwrecked sailors.

Bubbles, a mermaid

1 Start with the head. Add the nose, mouth and dots for the eyes.

2 Draw in the body and tail.

you can do it!
Use a felt-tip for the outlines. Scribble the colours with various coloured oil pastels.

3 Add the hair, necklace and bikini top.

4 Add the arms and hands.

Splat-a-fact!

'The Little Mermaid' is a story written by Hans Christian Andersen.

Poppy, the Flower Fairy

1 Start with the head. Add a nose, a mouth and dots for the eyes.

2 Add the dress.

you can do it!

Use a graphite stick for the lines. Add ink washes. Sponge inks on or add a second coloured ink on top of an area that is still wet for extra effects.

Splat-a-fact!

There are fairies all around us but they are so small that only children can see them.

3 Draw in the arms and legs.

4 Add hair, wings and a collar.

Princess Oceana

1 Start with the head. Add the mouth and two dots for the eyes.

you can do it!

Use wax crayons for texture and paint over it with watercolour paint. Use felt-tip for the lines.

2 Add the body, bikini top and beads.

3 Draw in the hair and a crown.

4 Draw the long, curved tail.

5 Add the arms.

Splat-a-fact!

Mermaids keep their tails shiny by rubbing them daily with seaweed.

Melody, a mermaid

1 Start with the head. Add nose, mouth and dots for the eyes.

2 Add her hair.

you can do it!

Draw the outline with felt-tip and colour it in with pastel pencils.

Splat-a-fact!

Mermaids can live for 300 years.

3 Add the bodice and beads.

4 Draw in the arms and hands holding a harp with four strings.

5 Add the tail and a rock.

The Fairy Princess

1 Cut out the wings. Stick down.

you can do it!

Cut out shapes from coloured paper. Stick them onto a sheet of paper as shown. Use a felt-tip for the face.

2 Cut out hair and dress. Stick down.

3 Cut out head and arms. Stick down. Add nose, mouth and eyes with felt-tip.

4 Cut out crown, legs and shoes. Stick down.

Splat-a-fact!

A 'fairy ring' is a circle of toadstools where the fairies gather to dance.

MAKE SURE YOU GET AN ADULT TO HELP YOU WHEN USING SCISSORS!

Holly, the Christmas Fairy

1 Start with an oval for the head. Add eyes, nose and a mouth.

2 Add the shape of the hair.

3 Draw the body and dress.

4 Add arms holding a present.

5 Draw the legs and feet.

6 Add bows to the hair and parcel.

7 Finish by adding the wings.

You can do it!

Use wax crayons for texture and paint over it with watercolour paint. Use felt-tip for the lines.

Splat-a-fact!

Titania, Queen of the fairies, lives in a fairy castle with her husband, King Oberon.

Pebbles, a mermaid
1
Start with the head. Add nose, mouth and dots for eyes.
2 Add the hair and beads.
3 Draw in the bodice and tail.
you can do it!
Use a felt-tip for the lines. Add colour using chalky pastels. Use your fingers to blend the colours.
Splat-a-fact!
Mermaids are beautiful creatures that are half human and half fish.
4 Add the arms and the rock.
5 Draw in her hair clasp and comb.

Twinkle, a fairy

1 Start with the head. Add the nose, mouth and dots for the eyes.

2 Draw in the neck and hair.

3 Add the dress.

You can do it!

Use marker pens to fill in the background and to add colour details. Use a felt-tip for the lines.

Splat-a-fact!

A fairy always carries a pinch of magic dust to help with her spells.

4 Draw in arms and legs.

5 Add a wand and wings.

Ella, the Dust Fairy

1 Start with the head. Add mouth, nose and dots for eyes.

2 Add the dress.

3 Draw in the hair and arms.

You can do it!

Use wax crayons to create patterns and texture. Paint over it with watercolour paints. Use a felt-tip for the lines.

4 Draw in the feather and the legs.

5 Add two wings.

Splat-a-fact!

Not all fairies have wings. Some fairies don't fly at all.

Index

www.salariya.com
where books come to life!
FREE APP!
Download our free iPhone and iPad catalogue app. Search for Salariya or Book House
Available on the App Store
SALARIYA
Follow us on Facebook and Twitter
www.youtube.com/user/BookHouse100
Scribblers
THE BOOK HOUSE BLOG
The Book House blog - competitions, giveaways and current news
Children's non-fiction and graphic novels
Scribo fiction
Fiction for children and teenagers
FREE WEB BOOK!
Free activities, puzzles and web books, with information about our books for babies, toddlers and pre-school
FREE WEB BOOKS!
Four free web books
iPhone and iPad are registered trademarks of Apple Inc.